Butterfly Breathe

Never Be Afraid to Fly

Butterfly Breathe

Never Be Afraid to Fly

Kendra Benford

Printed in the United States of America

First Printing, 2018

ISBN-13: 9781947656642

ISBN10: 1947656643

The Butterfly Typeface Publishing
PO BOX 56193
Little Rock Arkansas 72215

Dedication

To my grandfather and mother

"If you don't believe in yourself, no one else will. God gives His toughest battles to His strongest soldiers. Don't give up yet; God always has you regardless!"

-Kendra "Niki" Benford

Table of Contents

Foreword

My grandfather and I would often have conversations over the phone about me "...using my gift before I lose it." I explained to him that I just wrote for fun and to express myself when I feel like no one listens to me.

Grandfather continued to preach about why I should write.

Unfortunately, when I finally gave consideration to what he was saying, he passed away from cancer.

Like grandfather, my mother urged me to write as well. My mother also passed away, and she too will not see my talent grow into what she and grandfather knew in their hearts it would be.

Mother gives me the motivation to keep moving forward.

Acknowledgments

I would like to thank my family and friends who continually help me strive for greatness.

I would also like to give a special thanks to Ms. Iris Williams for believing in me and giving my poetry a chance to inspire others.

Bet

I'm worried out of my mind
trying to believe in the saying,
"Everything takes time,"
but quite often asking God, "When
will it be my time to shine?"

In love with the potential of a man in
my dreams,
that's why I take the low blows even
though they are exposed
to be really mean.

My mind often takes a walk
down a memory
that sometimes my heart
is more concerned

that this might be

a waste of pure energy.

I wanted to be treated

with love so bad,

that I accept the reflection of what I

once had,

that when I look

at my perception of love now,

I can't help but get sad.

So, I accept bad habits to expose what

I'm feeling

because in my mind,

I think that its causing healing.

If anything, it numbs my pain.

Sex or drinking,

that's what helps this pain.
My heart has drained so much;
I don't think it has anything
left to gain.

Too afraid to try something new
because all I ever wanted
and knew was you.

Verbal abuse is just like physical. The
only difference
between the two,
is it gives you mental damage.
All I think I'm doing
is building up more baggage.

There is a difference between good
attention and bad attention.

With me overthinking
between the two,
gives me more tension.

Being in love or being loved for the
night,
after thinking on it,
I don't know which one
seems right.

I know, in my heart, I'm a queen, and
a big part is missing
in my dreams.

How I display my actions
makes my body throw out
hoe-ish transactions.

How I see things is not what I get, so I

take life

as an unreliable bet.

Christmas Mom

It's that time of year
where people meet with cheer.
But I can't
because my heart
is building up with fear
because I know that you
will no longer be here.

I feel you in the air,
but it still doesn't seem fair.
Why does God always want
my heart to tear?
Didn't He know
we were the perfect pair?

That was how I felt back then, when I
thought there was no more room left
for me to bend.

At times, when I get sad,
I think about all the awesome times
we had,
and I sometimes share them
with dad.

I hate that you had to go away,
but I guess God knew
you couldn't stay.

This was your favorite
time of year,
so I am determined
to put on my best gear.

Your smile is what I miss,
and that's something I wish
I could put
on this year's Christmas list.

"I love you poo," is what I would
always hear you say,
and now, it sucks
that I have to remember you
this way.

People don't realize
how good they have it,
and Mommy, since you left,
I have become a silent savage.

Don't worry;
I still have a good heart.

I just have to adjust
to this new start.

Everyone is fine,
just missing you
one day at a time.

I still do
because I felt the only one
who understood me, was you.

But daddy's still here,
and he'll keep me in check.
Trust and believe,
if something ever were
to go wrong,
he knows to yell,
"All hands on deck."

I'm telling you, "Merry Christmas" to
the high heavens above,
and even though we don't always
understand His reasons,
trust and believe me,
you can bet God does.

Decisions

A poem from my mind
exited from my heart;
sometimes desiring a new start.

Love is hard to keep
because sex has become easier to
find.
But with all relationships
and friendships,
it comes down to being
based on time.

Stay strong in the love
of the company you keep.

Never put lust ahead
to get a quick nut in
the next person's bed.

The best love held
is held near and dear to yourself,
and keep the rest on a shelf.

Trying something new,
"Yeah, I'm down for the cause,"
but I'm just not ready
for the damages that will happen
when I fall.

If men, just like women,
would take care of home,

it would then leave room
for the significant other

to stand tall.
And the other wouldn't have to
worry about losing them at all.

Getting too involved or invested
into someone who knows
they're not ready,
just leaves you in harm's way
and a little unsteady.

Exploring each other
even though it sounds tempting
and exciting,
I just don't want to make myself
too inviting.

My heart speaks volumes
while my body wants touch
in value.

I'd be lying
if I said I didn't want it
or wonder just as much as you,
but my heart normally tells me
what to do.

If someone's heart is not in it,
why even try?

Experiencing it if you can't have
the full expectation,
I want true dedication
and to be someone's motivation.

Many times, I wondered
about friends with benefits too,

and that however,
it's true,

but I also have a sound mind
and heart too.

Venerable to a tee,
but all I have left is me.

My daddy raised a queen
not someone's one night or booty
call.
If I can't be treated like that,
then I don't need it at all.

Getting to know you is cool
but that's all I'm trying
to give to you.

If something changes
along the way,

then it shows
you were meant to stay.

Changed behavior shows
a person's character.

I like the new her
who looks back at me
because that means
I passed the test.
I still smile with the best.

Grown as to what I know I need,
I just need help
finding someone to take the lead.

Mommy's no longer here;
so, she can't hug me
or wipe my tears.

She left and whispered,

"Face your fears."

A Love Worth Dying For

Ambitious, confident, full of
wisdom, all of those
I once carried,
until the day
I agreed to be married.

Didn't know my future would later
on cause me to miscarry and finally
be early buried.

Fighting back has always been a
misguide to me,
because in my heart the good
I would always see.

A wife to be
and the perfect family life,
yes that sounded about right,
but being awaken to black eyes and
bruised skin-
who is this woman
that lies within?

There is no way I will let this man
back in,
but unfortunately, I did.
The only thing it took was an
apology with flowers,
and that was always my
happily ever after.

I prayed all the time that one day it
would stop,

and one day God gave me
my last shot.

I was happy and felt free
because I had a baby
waiting for me.

I was pregnant, and it was his, but I
would often wonder did I finally
win?
Everyone told me to leave or fight
back,
I did, then God decided
to take my angel back.

"Stress," the doctor says.
So then I began to think,
"Him or me?"

And wondered
is this how it will be?

One night I finally got the courage
to leave,
but he had other plans
up his sleeve.

Life support is where I was
as the doctor's last words to my
family was,
"I think it's time
we pull the plug."

God had a plan and He created it
just for me,
I am flying free and happy to be just
my daughter and me.

Valuable Lessons

Saying goodbye

to childish moments and thoughtless

tears

as we say farewell

to our negative fears,

Learn to love hard

and love strong.

Trust me, one day

you will find where you belong.

Growing up, you learn a lot.

but you always
have to remember
what you've been taught.

Be wise of the company you keep;
you never want to fall in too deep.

Don't make promises in the dark
because that's how people begin to
lose the sparks.

Don't hold on to words so tight; you
never know who could be telling the
story right.

The one thing that I have learned is
to trust with an open heart,
but do not wear it on your sleeve.

You never know
if they're being sneaky
or just preparing to leave.

Always see
and believe you're beautiful,
and know that there is someone out
there,
To Have and To Hold.

You just have to keep the faith and
be strong.

I learned my lesson,
as hurtful as it was,
but what can you do when the
damage has already been done?

I kept myself going
and have my mind set
that "GOD"
is not finished with me yet.

Try to do better
and make wiser choices,
is what I decided to do.
My question is this:
What's the plan for you?

Lost

Being lost
then finding yourself
makes you feel like
the greatest champ of all time.
All you needed
was that one moment to shine.

2016 was a rough one;
now, everyone calls me
the tough one.

Fragile heart, brutal mouth,
I guess I get that
from being in the south.

Missing my mom
like a fire without their pit,
I just wish someone
would've warned me
about how hard this pain
would hit.

Never afraid of being alone,
I am just drained
from being so strong.

The love I once believed in
is no longer there;
so, as pathetic as this may sound I've
decided to share.

I've accepted in my heart
that certain ways
will never change.

That's why I always say,
"This life will never be the same."

I deprive myself from a lot
that I deserve
because I am tired
of hearing
what I've already heard.

Sex is good to all
that's why; people make love seem so
dull.

Mommy always said,
"Never carry baggage that is already
dead."

Dreaming of a wedding gown, then
reality hits
that Mom Dukes won't be around.

A heart that's still golden,
I just wonder sometimes,
"Will I ever be chosen?"

Waiting sucks
because it almost
makes you feel stuck.

Applications to date,
just not quite sure
what would be my fate.

I had connections with a few
just don't know
which ones are true.

Babies are all I see;
it just sucks that no one ever takes a
chance on me.

I fought for everything I've had,
so why do I still feel so sad?

Suicidal thoughts I beat,
but yet, I still feel
I got a fatal cheat.

Many blessings
are to come my way;
I just hope this time around someone
stays.

Love me right or not at all,
because I can stand tall
in this life, on my own.

Because unlike many,
I am never afraid to be grown.

Just My Imagination

Just my imagination
to think that my love was ever going
to be good enough
to change you
as you question me as to why I linger
for someone new.

Crying at night,
praying to God that everything would
be all right.
Forgetting my voice
and who I once was often.
So how my story goes,

my head got harder,
while my butt continues to soften.

Just my imagination to take action in
my own satisfaction.
Too bad my heart doesn't give
in to those kinds of transactions.

Men are like fish,
too many in the sea,
but I still don't understand why
I continually let this one man
use me.
It's almost as if I am
his favorite tea.

Just my imagination longing for the
touch of my mom's hugs.
That's when I knew

I was dreaming,
as my heart aches and tugs.

Some people will hold on to
disrespectful relationships,
just to make one memory last.
But you got to remember,
you can't chase your past.

Crown

Battered and beaten
yet still no one listens.

They're too full of friction
to even mention
the beauty of motivation.

Sorry has become
an apology blocker,
respect has become
the egotistical stalker.

And love, unfortunately,
is caught in between

because it does not like
being mean.

Respect grows you;
it never tries to put a damaging hold
on you.

Respect never get
its honorable credit
because the people place love
as their debit.

Trust gets trashed;
that's how most relationships don't
last.
People are too focused
on their irrelevant past.

Love is beautiful,

but respect is better
as it states on the engravement
of my comfortable sweater.

The heart can be renewed,
if people cared enough
to hold on to you.

With every tear that drops,
it screams uncertain fear
that people are afraid to hear.

People would rather be in love than
to stand proud alone,
when you should be fearless
at the crown you own.

FREE

Have you ever loved so hard
to the point that you were numb?
Embarrassed at the thought
that everyone was thinking
you're being dumb?

Hurt beyond imagine
almost like when children
had their hopes up
for watching magic.

I embrace what I want
but am consistently deprived
of what I deserve.

That is why I feel
that I am not being heard.

My career life is flying high.
Why, unfortunately,
does my personal life
feel like it wants to die?

Beautiful face,
with intelligence to match,
who in their right mind wouldn't
want that?

Loyal to a tee
and still no one wants me.

Disrespected at the most, sometimes,
I would sit
and wonder how much

all my love given

and not returned, will cost?

The person who's normally there, I

would just go to lie down

and stare.

Place my secrets that I know

my heart is not capable to bare.

Soul stolen and heartbroken

that's why I've become

brutally outspoken.

I fall to my knees and pray at night

that God blesses me

just to be treated right.

Tired is what I am

because people cannot take me being

real;
so, they walk away
being unable to deal.

Until this day,
my heart isn't healed;
so, I place it in a box
and leave it sealed.

What I see is true love,
family, and honesty.

I am trying my hardest
not to believe all that is fantasy.

So, I keep saying,
"Hold on, because God has
my full destiny."

Suicide Friend

Losing control,

trying to hold on to hope,

and pretending

that everything in my life

is awesome and dope.

To be honest,

I think it's a pitiful joke.

I feel like I am suffocating

on the outside

when I place a smile

on my somewhat amused face. Why

do I live in fear on the inside thinking

that there is someone always better
to take my space?

I can't escape my jail cell,
the place I call my mind.

It got so bad
that suicide blocked up
most my time,
figuring out different ways
of control.
So, I can finally be relieved
of this hold.

Cutting was a thing I sold
my soul to,
my little secret
that never was told.

Insecurities beat me
while I rattled my mind
on being free
because I strongly believe
no one truly cares about me.

Wanting to find love
but always hitting a dead end,
"Damn! Why can't I win?"

Beautiful woman
who no one sees,
now stands a verbally brutal beast is
what society made me be.
So my blade and I become a 'we'.

Sometimes at night
when everyone's asleep,
me and my little friend talk.

And I silently say,
"Maybe this time,
I'll make the cut deep."

Doubt

I hear your whispers at night telling
me not to give up
without a fight,
but honestly,
ever since you left
nothing has really felt right.

I am always finding reasons
to cop out
because everything I once believed
in I now doubt.

A personality sent from grace
to match this beautiful face,
but now, I couldn't care less

and am hungrier
for increased space.
Mommy, I don't want to win
this useless race.

I am so used to being put second
and not really heard
that sometimes I wish to fly away like
a bird.

I don't want to point the finger
for my own self-pity or misery.
I just don't want my heart
to repeat history.
So, I remain to myself
and hold on to that mystery.

A smile that fools many
in an insecure girl

who knows she maybe
a bit skinny.

With a pain that can't be erased from
the rain,
it's a wonder how I remain sane.

I once believed
there was nothing I couldn't do
as long as I always had you.

A career, marriage and kids,
hey my future was all there,
but now, all I feel for life
is a humorous dare.

Mommy told me,
"Life isn't always fair."
But I say to her,

as I kneel at her grave,
"Why couldn't you get the chance to
be there?
Missing you really sucks.
Staying strong on my own
makes me feel alone.
So, what do I have
to call my home?"

I wake up the next morning
and sadly
repeat the same song.

Tamed Heart

A baby is what I crave;
I even get butterflies
every now and again
when I hear your name.

It just frustrates me
when were not on the same page.
I don't want to stand alone
on this huge stage.

A future is what I see
if you would only take the time out to
listen to me,

and please, just once,
stop disrespecting me if you claim we
were meant to be.

Your useless responses,
filled with empty promises,
cut deep like a knife;
so, I let you beat me down
with your selfish heart
through the fight
hoping you will finally
gain your sight
to know what's right.
That way, I can finally sleep without
tragic nightmares creeping through
the night.
But I guess that's too much to ask,
right?

I've got the mind
of a strong woman,
with all qualities attached,
as you took them for granted
and had the audacity to ask,
"Why did you run away from me and
never look back?"

I replied saying,
"If I didn't,
then I would've fallen off track, and I
know for a fact
my mommy would've never wanted
that."

Saying goodbye is never easy,
and I don't mean to sound
like Chris "Breezy,"

but I had to when I had to look up
and tell mom
to, "Rest easy."

I love you,
and that will never change,
but I can't stick around
if you're going to continue
the same game.

I want to attract beautiful
not walk around in shame,
and baby, be honest with yourself.
Maybe your heart
just can't be tamed.

Amazing Grace

There is not one day that goes by that
I don't think about
your little hands and feet,
praying to God every night
that one day we will meet.

Sometimes, I feel
that you are already there,
and when reality sets in,
the truth is too hard to bear;
which sometimes
makes me scream that,
"Life isn't fair."

God has a perfect timing
for everything
even when we don't understand
anything.

I believe God wants a good life
for this soon to be mommy;
so, I don't have to beg, borrow, and
plead
just to gain a little extra money.

Your mommy has so many dreams
that sometimes I don't even know
what half of them mean,
but I know you will be
my number one
who will make this whole team.

Grandma would've loved you
if she got the chance to be here,
but she is the one
who taught mommy
to dream with no fear.

Mommy didn't always
make the best decision
because ninety percent
of the time,
I was stuck in deep confusion.

Mommy prays
that when you are born,
you are never like that.
Always believe with facts,
and never let anyone
make you get off track.

All *this* mommy knows

is I cannot wait to see

your beautiful face,

and maybe then,

I will make a believer

out of someone

because that will truly be

God's amazing grace.

A Memory to Remember

A beautiful strong black woman with
long legs
and mediocre thighs,
oh yeah,
I remember her personality
was too extravagant to hide.

And believe me when I say
she was one of a kind.
If you if got out line,
trust me,
she was never too afraid
to test your behind.

My mother had a smile
that would brighten up a room when
she walked in;
brown eyes so mysterious
you would think it's a sin.

I write these memories
in the sky
praying that my Father above
will graciously tell her for me
that I said, "Hi"
and to express my regret
because I wasn't ready
for her to die.

But, I believe that night
God whispered to her and said,
"It's your turn to fly."

Even though she pleaded wondering
why
she couldn't say, "Goodbye."

God said back,
"My child, give it time; everyone will
grow later
to understand
My many reasons why."

My mommy was funny and
sometimes a little mean.
Everyone always said,
"Don't worry,
she just want to be seen."

Mommy, I tell you all my future
accomplishments and also the little
secrets I hold because I know that

even on your last breath, you'll never
tell.

If anything, you'll scream from the
clouds and say,
"Baby, give them hell.
My poo is going to be something one
day."

That's what she
would always say.
I just really wish God gave her a free
pass to stay.

Your son is doing great.

Your mother misses your embracing
face,

but one thing we all know is that no
one will ever take
Minnie Ann Caldwell's place.

So, until we meet again,
I'll leave it at "Hello, mother,"
until you can finally say back to me…
"Hello, daughter."

Reflection

On the outside looking in,
people see someone
they believe I hold within.

I hold a lot of different qualities than
what my image is sold.
One true fact
is that I have a heart of gold.

Strong woman, I am, and I do know
the value of my worth.

That's why most men
do not cherish,

and they end up
in a world of perish.

I am well formed in every way
of life's design.

Sexy, independent, intelligent,
and loyal.

I am queen
who has never been treated
with royal define.
It is okay
because at the end of it all,
I will remain
to have my own mind.

What you see is what you get.
I never change up to make someone
else's perfect fit.

Looking for another like me,
never because I am one of a kind.

I can't be something I'm not.
If you want it that easy,
go find yourself a thot.

My mama raised a queen
not to be with someone to be seen.
I'm not being mean;
I just see the beauty in my dream.

No money is needed to please me
because I got that on my own,

and I'm never afraid
to stand alone.

Give me orgasms
through your words
coming from your mind
not just between my legs
at any given time.

Heavenly made and obsessive with
self,
disability or not,
I am way too valuable
to be put back on the shelf.

From Auntie

My little ones
are the breath that I breathe.

You guys are the many reasons that
make me.
To your little hands
to your tiny feet,
I' am so thankful God wanted us to
meet.

"Stop. Put that down,"
I yell.
But I couldn't image life,
without you guys around.

When 'TT' is sad,
ya'll are the ones
that make my day seem
not that bad.

I try my best to help raise
you guys to be kind and strong, but
to also realize when something is
wrong.

Apologize when needed,
but never apologize
for being you,
but keep in mind -
to be better
than what you see me do.

I know ya'll miss grandma and 'TT"
does too,

but remember there is always a

piece of her

that lives

inside you.

Remember that part is true,

and never forget

that 'TT' will always love you.

Wishful Thinking

The nights I lay on your chest,
I think to myself,
"There is no other feeling that speaks
best."

But as I lay beneath your arms, I
breathe and begin to wonder,
"Is there a coward that lurks behind
this scene?"

Embraced by the warmth of your
hug, thinking out loud,
"How can I ever neglect this love?"

The kindest charm with the

infectious smile,

hell, with a human that addictive

I wouldn't mind walking

a thousand miles

for as my heart

takes its time to restore.

Sometimes,

he reaches for my highest climax.

With the surround sound,

for a moment,

I see no one but us around.

But I won't lie.

The more I let him in,

I slowly break down,

and I swear on my life
sometimes that this is nothing
but pure sin.

That's why I constantly
turn the other cheek
and let it win.

but I'm really at a lost,
and I don't know
how much more
I can possibly bend
when all I ever needed
was time to spend.

"I love you,"
the most deceitful words spoken
because if that were true,

my respect would've been chosen.

Love so consuming
makes me wonder
who else are you amusing.

Intense
when our two bodies align,
I blind myself to see
every disrespectful sign, infatuated
by you
that my star faded its shine.

Open thighs
meeting half way
as you fearfully back off and say,
"Sorry, I wasn't meant to stay."

Many thoughts race in my mind.

I wonder, "Did I push something that
wasn't meant to be?"
Then, I think, "It's not my fault. You
couldn't handle me."

Denying what you feel
doesn't help when you,
despite all odds,
know this is real.

Invisible Apology

I loved you over and over maybe
more than I thought I should,
but hey, I believed in you more than
you thought I would.

A love I chose to go back to because I
knew on God there would be no one
who could replace you.

Building every scar on my back
because I didn't draw a line
called respect which unfortunately
you lack.

Sadly, I don't blame you.

I fought me

in believing that one day

you and I could be.

My best friend, my pinky,

the one I felt was true blue,

now I'm feeling empty

because I don't know what to do or

say

every time I look at you.

Wish you well in all your success,

I always told you

that you deserve the best.

Let God handle the rest.

But, this walking around

in brutal silence is killing me when all

I ever asked of you
was honesty.

Even though I feel we were supposed
to be a we,
I can't wait around for many more
years just to accept
your invisible apology.

Trapped

Reflection on the wall,
I yell at it and say,
"I'm not a waiting doll."

As it laughs back at me
and says, "You might as well be
because you too afraid
to let go and fall."

I'm enraged, so I yell louder,
"I'll show you,"
but cowardly inside,
I know what's true.

Beautiful, confident, and strong
seeping out
but inside filled with doubt,

ladies and gentlemen,
I introduce you to self-doubt.

You take that and mix it with
depression;
only then,
you'll learn your life lesson.

That was all me
because I had no idea
what my purpose could be.

I never felt a reason to fight
until I got blessed
with all my little ones overnight.

Children show you
what life is about.
That's why I finally released
my self-doubt.
I looked up, and God whispered, "You
found your way out."

Soul Ties

Funny how life works
to capture someone's soul,
then another one gains a heart,
kind of ironic,
when I think of the thought.

When the bodies align together we
as humans think we found the
perfect treasure.

Life can go like math,
it can end with a positive
or a negative,
depending how long
the situations last.

You are mine to hold,
as I was yours to keep.
Some nights I still find it hard
to sleep.

Drawn to it like Adam to his Eve, I
just wish I knew all the lies
that were hidden
between the sleeves.

When a soul is taken
it's locked into one's mind,
which makes it hard
to eventually break ties.

Dancing in my Own Silence

Dancing in my own silence because I
knew we were wrong,
but I have no one else to blame but
me
because I continued to repeat
the same song.

Dancing in my own silence
when everyone was around because I
was afraid my cries would make too
much of a sound.

Dancing in my own silence because I
have no more love
to show.

I dream of potentially being
my only, "Way to go!"

Dancing in my own silence because I
miss my mother's kindness.

Dancing in my own silence because
I'm tired of breaking my heart,
even when I try giving myself
a new start.

Dancing in my own silence because I
will soon have victory and start
prospering on track.
I've been through way too much hell
to even think of looking back.

Dancing in my own silence because
being the woman I am and how far

I've grown,

I realize that life is easier

once you finally dance alone.

Letter

I saw something
I didn't want to see
that made me question
the value of you and me.
I wasn't in an abusive relationship,
but hell, might as well be.

I was taking verbal punches
to the face,
and sadly I label that
as my best luck.

I was manipulated
on endless accounts

to the point where I suffocate
in self-doubt.

This note applies to myself,
kids, and everything else
down the line
including my family issues combined.

Scars so deeply embedded,
yet you still have the nerve to ask,
"Why do you feel so defeated?"

I place a mask on daily
because I don't want people to see
the weight I cautiously carry.

I'm dead inside,
so I rarely see the need to try.

Suicidal note beside my bed
because I cannot release the words
you said.

They were too hard to bare as you
gasp for air.

As you read the last line
of my letter...

"Now do you care?"

Sight

Lost soul, sound mind
if only people understood
that life moves by time.

Hurt people, hurt people.

Love with a passion,
hell, that should be illegal
while people in full relationships
while still carry a mindset
of single and ready to mingle.

Main chicks claiming that side chicks
need to know their place; all the

while that man allowed the other
women to take that space.

Now, you sit and wonder,
"Do I really want to continue this
destructive race?"

No morals in sight,
that's why the most loyal people find
it hard to sleep at night.

The heart is strong,
but you can't trust anyone
to protect it
because every time
you give to someone,
it constantly gets neglected.
That's just my point of view. "What is
your perspective?"

Listen up

Black people,
"What are we doing,"
because every time
I look on the news
we are constantly losing.

I'm all the way with the cause of
black lives matter,
but the question is,
"Do you think your life matters?"

The roles have changed completely.

Now, black men don't even question
work

when they have a woman
who works all day.

Then, tired
but still gets energy to cook
while some black men
won't even think twice
to pick up a book.

Women will be better off
if they put that much effort
into raising their children
as well as their men.

But, people we have to do better. It's
not just black men;

some black women
have these issues too.

Doesn't the world remember the

saying,

"Monkey see monkey do."

The changes

have to come from you.

Growing Pain

My love, my heart, my trust,
it's funny how one moment can
evaporate that into dust.

Trusting in a man
instead of holding God's hand, that's
why I now feel like I'm drowning in
the devil's quicksand.

I was so quick to plan
out my own life
that I really didn't care about
who was wrong
and who was right.

The day my mother was buried
I felt like my life had no room
to be carried;
so, I started living it by me
which means not so scary.

A little pleasure here and there and
someone to say I love you, that seems
pretty fair.

Your body is a temple;
it's not supposed
to be treated simple.

Feeling your heart shatter is one
heavy pain to feel,

but that's the only way hard headed

people learn

that God is real.

Healed me from the inside out, now, I

do not take for granted what my life

can be about.

Dear Mommy

How are you today?
I came to visit
because I have a lot to say.

I let go of the man
you told me to,
not because his love wasn't true; I
just got fed up with the hell
he was taking me through.

Sadly, I know you would say,
"I told you, but mommy's love will
always stay."

Mommy,
honestly I was angry with you

for a while,
so I started playing Russian roulette
because I felt it was unfair that you
were gone,
and I wanted to play
in heaven too.

I learned my lesson quick
when I got checked for a baby, the
doctor hit a miss.

"I can't win for loosing,"
you always said,
as I cried silently for months
in my bed.
My question I ask daily,

"What is my success
without you?"

If you saw me now,
you wouldn't recognize me.
After you died,
life and people had a funny way of
changing me
from who I *thought* I'd be.

There are moments
where I urge to call you,
imagining you would finally answer
to say
none of this that happened
was true.

But you're not.
Unfortunately that moment
only exist in my thought.

I love you
and miss you every day.
I question God as to
why you couldn't stay.
Too bad you can't take this
replaying nightmare away.

Mommy, I have envy in my soul and
resentment in my heart. That's why
in one moment in my mind,
I wished death
became my new start.

You, Nana, and Daddy taught me
how to carry strength, love, and

compassion,
but lately some days,
all I crave is
getting evil satisfaction.

Yea I know what you're thinking,
"This girl is not you,"
Well mommy I am sorry
but death, love, and life can
immediately change you.
Plus, I don't have you to tell me
what's the best thing to do.

I smile my best
when I get up to prepare
for another life test.
God helps to try and put my mind at
rest.

I don't listen much
cause I am mostly consumed with
missing your touch.

Just showing my Benford honesty - I
tried to do things
to spite you;
just to win an invisible argument,
like we always use to do.

Mommy I was so mad with you and
God, I could've sued.
I did everything right
and I still lost you.

But I figured out a plan and
hopefully by prayer,
it'll come true.

Cause I am tired of fighting

my God

and I really,

from my little drained heart - miss

you.

Invisible Women

When I look at you now
I don't even see me,
I see everything
I never wanted to be.

Scars from every direction.
I think I finally learned
God's valuable lesson.

For years I was tied in emotional,
unbearable chains trying to blame
someone
for my self-inflicting pain.

Fighting to stop the cycle

was a drag,

so I stuffed everything

in a private feelings bag.

Trying to reconcile

with this thing I call love

made me feel like I was drowning

and could not find

my way above.

I hate you

because I was selfish

with my body

for the things you made me do.

But it's not just my body,

I hate it's my heart too.

It's too big to allow people

to continuously hurt me
the way they do.

Invisible women
no longer taking control
over my life
because I now look at that woman
and see
a soon to be wife.

Proud and strong,
ready to take on everything
as life slowly moves along.

Yes I see the growth in me waving
goodbye
to the one I use to be.
Some days,
I feel my mommy's smile

and I believe

now she is truly proud of me.

Man I Used to Know

Seeing you for who you are
makes me sad
because even though
people doubted us,
I knew we
were meant to be.

A husband and a family with love,
yes, that's what made me proud. That
was my answer every time someone
asked me "Why do you stick around?"

A man who was caring, playful, and
never let me down,
but over the years I felt like he was

self-observed and always left me to
drown.

Disrespected to say the least and yet
again always getting placed in the
back seat,
love doesn't hurt,
"So why did I accept hurtful things
with no strength to fight back?"

Because I prayed
that it would stop and finally bless us
to get back on track,
I learned the hard way
that I won't ever get that back.

So, instead of loving him,
I finally decided to love me more,

even if that meant me crying

as I walked out the door.

My Very Last Day

July 6th 2016
plays like a horror film constantly
in my head.
While most days I struggle
to get out of bed.

I can still see
if I focus in
on what my heart
can never mend.

The cries and screams
are still so clear to me
not in a million years
I would plan this life to be.

Make a family, be a wife,
yeah that's how I dreamed
of my life.

2009-2016 the devil
has reaped hell
to where I never got a sincere "I'm
sorry" or "I wish you well".

It got so bad, to where everything I
try to grow, fails.
I have no feelings anymore,
cant you tell?
I suffocated my heart so much
to where it started to swell,
but I can hear God saying,
"If you don't stop, this is not going
to end well."

My mother was dead,

so sorry to say -

I was eager to write my letter

to hell.

Funny thing about God's love

is He never lets you go,

no matter what

and by His grace,

I was in luck.

He fought hard to give me peace

and He allowed

my anger to cease.

My mommy

still comes to visit

and we have our

mommy and me talks,

and it amazes me

in most of my dreams,

I can walk.

I still hear me saying,

"I'll see you tomorrow mommy," as

I always said calmly.

Until we meet again,

"I love you and I'll be thinking of my

very last day,

when you were here

and you stayed."

About the Author

Kendra Benford is 30, soon to be 31. She has cerebral palsy and graduated from FTCC with an Early Childhood degree. Her goal is to become a teacher's assistant.

Since the passing of her mother, Kendra has accomplished a lot. This book highlights the challenging emotions she endures over living on without her. Some challenges she has overcome, others she still struggles with.

The two-time author plans to build a productive business, write and sale inspiring and entertaining books. She also plans to become an amazing and loving foster parent in an effort to continue spreading unconditional love.

For Nana

Butterfly Typeface

Publishing

Contact us for all your

publishing & writing needs!

Iris M Williams

PO Box 56193

Little Rock AR 72215

501-823-0574